The End-Time Wealth Transfer

WE MUST PREPARE TO RECEIVE IT

I0517653

A Prophetic Word From Our Lord

Dan Boykin, ThM, DD, Prophet of God

HIGHERLIFE PUBLISHING

Oviedo, FL

Published by HigherLife Publishing & Marketing, Inc.
PO Box 623307, Oviedo, FL 32762, AHigherLife.com

Designed by Faithe Stephens

ISBN (Paperback): 978-1-964081-49-6
ISBN (eBook): 978-1-964081-50-2
Library of Congress Case Number: 1-14929854441

Printed in the United States of America.

Dedication

This book is dedicated
to June, a companion and friend, to the end....
and to the men and women who have
persevered in their faith for this outpouring
of wealth transfer to God's people.

Contents

Foreword #1

SOME MAY BE DRAWN to this book looking for the secret to riches or wealth, but you will receive more than just material things from this book. I have known Dan Boykin to be a gifted prophet since 1982. I have the greatest respect for him, his ministry, and his gift of prophecy. Many of the ministers around me have witnessed this true gift operating in him as well. I have the joy to call Dan Boykin a true personal friend.

His book, *The End-Time Wealth Transfer Is Coming*, is a true gold mine of Scripture and a new prophetic Word from the Lord. I could not put the book down. The whole book is written with a strong balance between the Word of God and "Thus saith the Spirit of the Lord" concerning the wealth transfer promised in the Scriptures. This book is edifying and encouraging; it also includes warnings to the body of Christ at this crucial time in history.

In this book, the prophet's forefinger is pointing at the body of Christ with surgical precision concerning the promise of the wealth transfer when we sacrifice and are obedient to God's Word, as instructed in Scripture.

Read this book, and let's all get in line with this Word!

"The silver is mine, and the gold is mine, saith the LORD of hosts." —Haggai 2:8 (KJV)

Susan J. Williams
Attorney at Law, Winter Park, Florida

Foreword #2

I HAVE READ DR. Dan Boykin's book, *The End-Time Wealth Transfer Is Coming*, and I am excited about this revelation. Personally, I have predicted for eleven years that a transfer of wealth was about to happen. I believe this book shows us how it will come to pass.

It is written from a prophetic view; therefore, it is filled with symbolism. You will want to read it at least twice, as I did.

The "time of correction" for those who have strayed is already underway. Now is the time to repent and live a godly life. I believe the Holy Spirit will speak to you as you read this book. Clarification will come with prayer.

God bless you, and God bless Dr. Dan Boykin for sharing this Word from the Lord.

Dr. Daniel J. Tyler
President, International Seminary,
Plymouth, Florida

Foreword #3

I HAVE KNOWN DAN Boykin for more than forty years. In that time, he has shown himself to be a dedicated believer, steadfast in the Word, honest in ministry, and reliable in prophecy. He is never flippant when ministering to the body through preaching, word of knowledge, or prophecy. He has reached out to me and my family over the years with timely prophetic words of warning, as well as words of encouragement that were pivotal in our spiritual life.

I believe this book will serve as a spiritual warning and encouragement to those in ministry positions, as well as the entire body of Christ. As we take time to examine ourselves and our motives in ministry, we will be blessed, more effective, and better equipped to do our part in the end-time harvest.

Rachel King
Children's pastor; discipleship Ministries Director
for IPHC Sonshine Network Ministries; IPHC
Global Discipleship Ministries council member

Foreword #4

My wife (Debra) and I first met Prophet Boykin in the mid-1990s, and from that very first encounter, we knew he was extraordinary. We still remember him amid the construction of a new sanctuary—standing on scaffolding with a stream of blood running down his face—a powerful symbol of his unwavering commitment to God's Kingdom.

Over the years, Prophet Boykin has delivered prophetic words that have always proven accurate. He is not merely a teller of the Word; he is a doer of the Word—willing to sacrifice everything for the sake of truth. When he shared that he was writing down what God revealed to him, our spirits leaped for joy. As someone with the gift of giving, I have long yearned for a spiritual leader who would confront the mishandling of God's finances and speak boldly against the status quo.

Prophet Boykin's courageous revelations shine a light on the "golden calf" within the church—a wake-up call to those who have been worshiping the gift rather than the Giver. His timely insights have transformed our understanding of spiritual wealth and ignited a renewed passion for authentic, fiery faith.

We are profoundly grateful for his dedication to truth and for inspiring us—and countless others—to stand firm in our calling. This book is a must-read for anyone seeking to understand God's revelations in these challenging times.

Ed Campany
Florida business owner

Introduction

About This Prophetic Word from God

WHAT YOU ARE HOLDING in your hands is not your typical book; it is a direct word I received from the Lord. God has prepared a time of increase for His followers through a season of wealth transfer that has already begun.

The *end-time wealth transfer* is the redistribution of global wealth into the hands of those people who will use it to fulfill God's end-time purposes. To receive this wealth, we must prepare ourselves by honoring Him and by being responsible stewards of the resources He has given to us.

This is actually the second notable wealth transfer; the first one is documented in Exodus 12, which you can read about in chapter 11 of this book.

Proverbs 13:23 (KJV) says, "A good *man* leaveth an inheritance to his children's children: and the wealth of the sinner *is* laid up for the just."

In other words, people who honor God with their spiritual and physical gifts will receive His blessings in return. First, we must place our trust in God's faithfulness and promises instead of trying to attain wealth in sinful or unethical ways. And second, when He does bless us richly, we must use those gifts to glorify His Kingdom—not for our own pleasure or gain.

A time of revelation and correction must come into the lives of many, or they will not be able to receive this abundance.

This is a message of mercy and grace; God does not want anyone in His Kingdom to miss out on the coming blessings. He is giving us a chance to examine our lives as He lets us know who will be able to receive the great wealth transfer now getting underway. He wants us to prepare ourselves by living according to His plan and acknowledging that He is most important and that no sacrifice is too great for the Kingdom of God.

I encourage you to read this word. Digest it. Live by it. You will be blessed.

CHAPTER 1

The Assignment

IN THE VERY EARLY hours of October 22, 2024, I had an incredibly vivid and compelling dream that led me to convey an important message to the world that the Lord our God conveyed to me.

In the dream, I was attending a church service and was seated in the front row in the center of the sanctuary. Looking toward the platform, I watched for a moment as preparations were made for the service. People worked diligently to set up video and sound equipment, get musicians and singers in place, and perform other tasks to ensure everything would be just right.

It was then I noticed that, seated next to me on my left side, was a well-known minister dressed in a light-colored suit. God did not show me his face, so I did not know specifically who I was sitting next to, but I was certain he was a prominent minister with a large following. Because of the way the person in my dream was dressed, I assumed he was a male. However, that does not in any way limit this message to males. This person served as an illustration for us all. Holy Spirit revealed later to me why that person's identity was withheld.

For a few minutes, the minister to my left sat quietly, intensely watching the pre-service setup and preparation.

Suddenly, he became upset about something taking place on the stage. He stood quickly and headed to the platform, placing his right hand on my knee as though to push up from his seat. The ring on his finger caught my attention; it could not be ignored—a large, square, deep red ruby surrounded by diamonds. The gems were mounted into a brilliant gold setting that reached almost to the man's knuckle. It was a breathtaking piece that captivated my attention—until, that is, the unthinkable happened. I was not prepared for what I saw next.

As the minister rose to his feet and took a few steps forward, I looked up and saw that from his shoulders down to the top of his pants, his clothing was smeared with cow manure. Dung. The manure also covered the seat where he had sat next to me just moments before.

In that moment of astonishment over what I saw, I awoke from the dream.

Immediately, I heard the voice of the Lord: "I'm bringing Loyce home today." He was speaking of my spiritual mother and pastor, Loyce Rowland. And that day, Loyce passed into the arms of God. I did not realize it right away, but this, too, proved relevant to the message that would follow.

I knew the dream was from God, but its meaning was uncertain to me. Concern over what I saw and the need for clarity filled my heart and my prayers. I was instructed to write the vision down, to make it clear. That seemed like a peculiar instruction until I sat down with pen in hand. As I wrote, clarity came.

> *I knew the dream was from God, but its meaning was uncertain to me.*

Holy Spirit started to explain the message of the dream. He spoke little that first day, but over time, the vision itself became more vivid and unforgettable. Over the next few weeks, God continued to speak to me often, bringing clarity and revelation.

And then He gave me an assignment: He instructed me to write the message He was giving me for His church. Through this writing, I share that message with you.

CHAPTER 2

Too Many in This Condition

THE DREAM WOULD NOT leave me. Each time I thought about it or looked back over the paper on which I recorded it, it became more vivid. The weight of the message grew heavier in my spirit, yet I was uncertain about the overall word that God was urging me to speak.

My initial leading from Holy Spirit revealed that the dream is tied to the wealth transfer that God is going to bring about. The image I saw symbolized what has occurred already and what we can expect to happen if our hearts do not change.

I have discovered in my prophetic walk that the prophet's forefinger, when extended, represents one measure of grace. Choices are placed before us, along with the grace to choose wisely and see the decision through, if we only will. In the Bible, the phrase "finger of God" or "hand of God" represents God's direct intervention and power. In the fivefold ministry, discussed in chapter 5, the pointer finger, or index finger. is often associated with prophetic ministry. The prophet's finger points the way and guides people toward God's will.

Two days after the dream occurred, as I sat meditating on it once again, the Lord spoke clearly about the dung-smeared backside of the minister's clothing: "Many of My ministers are in this condition. They don't know it. They don't see it. I don't like it, and it should not be. But I continue to use them because the harvest is great, but the laborers are few."

> *The power that the calf holds over us is not the same for every person.*

He then brought a golden calf before my eyes. It was small at first but would grow larger and then, at times, shrink in size. The size of the golden calf represents its influence on us and the choices we make. The power that the calf holds over us is not the same for every person. And it can vary in our own lives if we are not consistent in our walk with God and if we allow our own priorities to become more important than His.

The Bible refers to a "golden calf" in the Old Testament, in Exodus 32, Deuteronomy 9:16, Nehemiah 9:18, and 1 Kings 12. It is an idol the Hebrews worshipped during the exodus from Egypt in the thirteenth century BC and during the age of Jeroboam I, king of Israel, in the tenth century BC. Worshipping a "golden calf" is viewed as a supreme act of idolatry and also of *apostasy*—the rejection of a faith once confessed.

All the while, this "golden calf" has been in the midst of the people, dumping dung on their backsides. They cannot see it, but others can. The dung represents many things that are unpleasing to God, including arrogance; pride; a lifestyle that goes beyond necessity; and the dross that comes forth when gold is heated, representing the impurities in us that must be removed from our lives.

Seeing the devastating effects of spiritual leaders' sin among us, many would say nothing out of fear, feeling they were not free to speak. Some tried to point the "manure" out to those wearing it, hoping they would clean themselves. Their words went unheard as the dung carriers covered themselves with a biblical blanket fashioned from the reproving words of God: "Touch not mine anointed..." (Ps. 105:15, KJV).

All the while, those smeared could not even smell the stench of the waste that followed on their backsides.

Too many are in this condition. May the Lord help us all. We all must change if we are to participate in the great and notable end-time wealth transfer.

CHAPTER 3

Caution Against Worshipping a "Golden Calf"

WHEN I WAS ABOUT twelve years old, several people from my church attended an A. A. Allen tent revival at the Orlando Fairgrounds. My father, younger sister, and I were in that group. The power of God's presence was evident throughout the service.

Evangelist Allen called for all the young people to come forward and receive prayer for their teeth. I did not respond, but my sister and many others did. I remember vividly a young man, probably around sixteen years old, who had several bad teeth. A. A. Allen prayed for the teen, who fell out under the power of God where he remained for close to half an hour. When he rose, there was not one bad tooth in his mouth. His teeth were new and solid.

My sister, still then a child, grew up never having a single dental problem. As a young woman, she could literally pop the cap off a soda bottle with her teeth. Ouch!

In the more than five decades that have followed that night, I have continued to witness, hear testimony of, and be a part of mighty moves of God through His anointed servants. Our God remains a God of miracles—in the physical, financial, emotional, and spiritual realms. Many of these anointed men and women continue in ministry or left this world humble and clean before God, regardless of the magnitude of their ministry or the financial blessing God bestowed on them.

Too many others, however, are now smeared with the dung of the golden calf. While they continue to operate in the anointing, the cry of their heart is, "More, more, more!" It is not a cry for more of God. It is instead a demand for more fame, more followers, and more wealth. They have evolved into one of those described in Proverbs 27:20: "Hell and destruction are never full; so the eyes of man are never satisfied."

They surround themselves with "yes men and women" who are afraid to speak the truth even if they recognize it, or they choose to ignore the truth because they want to be a part of the fanfare. They strive to maintain and increase their following through greater manifestations of the fire of God, but they don't teach the masses so they can continually carry the fire of God themselves.

These men and women of God have produced a golden calf in their lives. For some, it is a slow creation; for others, it is more rapid. One person's calf can be larger and produce more manure than another's. None are pleasing to God. They produce pollutants in ministries that God meant to be pure.

Aaron Creates a Golden Calf

So, how is a "golden calf" produced in the first place? Where does it come from? Scripture will enlighten us about this symbol of idolatry.

In Exodus 19, God calls Moses to go up to the mountain. Moses instructs the people to look to Aaron, who was his brother, and Hur for leadership until his return. In Exodus 20, God meets with Moses on the mountaintop and writes His law—the Ten Commandments—on tablets of stone so Moses can teach the people. Exodus 24 tells us that Moses was on the mountain for forty days and forty nights.

Chapter 32 of Exodus explains that the people did not expect Moses to be gone so long. They grew impatient with the delay in the law, or the Word of God, which was to instruct them, and a delay in the return of Moses, who was to lead them into the land of promise. They should have been headed to the land of milk and honey, yet there they were, still camped at Mount Moriah. They didn't even know what happened to Moses. Why should they have to wait any longer for the promise of God?

Aaron, a priest, was Moses's brother and three years older. Aaron was the first of the Levitical, or Aaronic, priesthood and was born to a family of Levites during Israel's enslavement in Egypt. In Exodus 4, God tells Moses that He will send Aaron with him to free the Israelites from Pharaoh.

Frustrated with Moses's delayed return, the Israelites went to Aaron and demanded of him, "Make us gods, which shall go before us..." (Exo. 32:33, KJV). The Hebrew people had grown accustomed to ancient Egypt's complex pantheon, consisting of between fourteen hundred and two thousand deities. This influence was evident in their request that Aaron make them gods to worship. Although they knew the God of heaven would be with them, they felt they needed other gods to lead, instruct, protect, and bless them.

Because Aaron grew up in an environment of idolatry, he likely witnessed idols being created in his early years. It's quite possible that his graving tool came from one of the smiths who forged these images. So, to appease the anxious Israelites, Aaron collected gold from them, melted it, and used his graving tool to fashion a golden calf in the likeness of the Egyptian bull god, Apis. Apis was the most revered of the bull gods and one of the most highly regarded gods of Egypt. It is taught that Apis was first honored as a fertility god.

Because Aaron grew up in an environment of idolatry, he likely witnessed idols being created in his early years.

However, as time went by, he became connected to other gods and associated with the power of pharaohs, the cycle of life and death, and the god of the underworld. It was believed that Apis assisted souls on their journey to the afterlife and gave them hope of resurrection. Also, because of his connection to other gods, many believed Apis to be a divine messenger and advocate between man and other gods.

This describes several characteristics of an antichrist spirit. It can come easily upon people who succumb to the pressure, often caused by delay, to produce wealth beyond their current level of anointing. When this happens, people enter a place of labor in a secular job, building their own kingdoms. They are looking beyond God's anointing, trying to accumulate more wealth to "keep up with the Joneses." Hebrews 13:5 (KJV) says, "Be content with such things as ye have." It is better for us to judge ourselves than to be judged by God.

Aaron had learned the art of graven images. He knew exactly how to construct a furnace and bring the fire to a temperature capable of melting all the gold pieces the people brought to him. He then created a large brick of gold from which he carved the calf.

Exodus 32:4 tells us, "After he had made it a molten calf [from gold]: and they said, These be thy gods, O Israel, which brought thee up out of the land of Egypt" (KJV, parenthetical phrase added). The power of the Lord God who delivered them out of bondage was attributed to gold fashioned into the image of a god their captors worshipped and credited with their captivity of God's people.

Aaron didn't stop with creating the calf. Verses 5 and 6 tell us that when Aaron saw it, he built an altar before it and shouted out a decree, "Tomorrow is a feast to the LORD" (Ex. 32:5, NKJV). The people rose up early the next day to offer burnt offerings and bring peace offerings, after which they sat down to eat and drink, and then they rose up to play.

The scene changes in verse 7 (NKJV) to reveal God's view of this action by the people. He says to Moses, "Go, get down; for your people, whom you brought out of the land of Egypt, have corrupted *themselves*."

Did they corrupt themselves through merriment or celebration? No, but the reason for their joy was in total disregard to God. The gold that God blessed them with to lift them up became their downfall because they worshipped it instead of Him, the giver.

We Must Remember That He Is the One Who Prospers Us

Jesus said His return will be as in the days of Noah. People will be eating and drinking and marrying, just like they did before the day Noah entered into the ark. As Noah was preparing the ark, the people were so engulfed in their pleasure that they did not hear the warning of God's servant. As a result, the flood came and took them all away.

I reemphasize that things are not wrong in themselves. God ordained feasts and celebrations in the Old Testament. Marriage is ordained of God. God wants us to take time to rest and refresh ourselves and enjoy things of this life.

The danger arises when these things are done in disregard for God and when we forget that it is He who prospers us and gives us the power, or ability, to obtain wealth (see Deuteronomy 8:1–20). We can attribute our own hard work or charisma for the means to do so. We can put our own pleasure ahead of God's instruction. We can use resources He provided for ministry to seek our own pleasure. However, these choices are not pleasing to God.

A trustworthy friend shared with me the account of a minister who would be flying home on a private jet only to change direction in midflight to enjoy a dinner in Italy or France. He spent thousands of dollars on one evening of pleasure. That's an example of the influence of the golden calf.

When God told Moses to go down from the mountain because the people had corrupted themselves, He explained, "They have turned aside quickly out of the way which I commanded them" (Ex. 32:8, KJV). Jesus made it very clear that He is the way (see John 14:6). If pleasure and prosperity by any means is more important to us than remaining in the way Jesus has ordained for us, we will soon be covered in the dung of a golden calf.

As believers, we should always remember where we came from. Our past should not consume us or hold us back, but it is equally dangerous to forget that it is by grace alone that we have been made new.

Paul is an excellent example of this principle. He didn't forget the man he was before Jesus, describing himself as the chief of sinners (see 1 Timothy 1:12–16). But he did not let the guilt or shame of his past stand in his way of ministry. He knew he was a new man in Christ and was willing to suffer many things for the Kingdom (see Philippians 3:13, 14; 2 Corinthians 5:17).

God is not slack concerning His promises, but too many times, we are slack in trusting Him. We experience delays and are unwilling to wait or to pay the price. Often, when we experience a delay, God is trying to get us to acknowledge what is in our

> *God is not slack concerning His promises, but too many times, we are slack in trusting Him.*

hearts. When we do, we will have a choice to make.

We can choose to heed the words of Hebrews 6:12 and follow those who, through faith and patience, inherit the promise. Or we can choose to seek other gods to expedite our journey. This is many times the very first step in creating a "golden calf"—an idol.

The creation of a golden calf often happens when we have not pursued the Word or previous instruction received from the Lord. It is then that we are prone to grow impatient and create a mess.

Thus was the heart of the people and the heart of Aaron, their priest.

Moses Intervened for the People, and God Withheld His Wrath

Moses remembered well the God who brought them out of bondage. When God told Moses what the people had done, he told Moses to step aside so He could execute His wrath upon them and consume them.

Moses interceded on their behalf. He asked God why He would execute such wrath against His own people, whom He brought out of Egypt with great power. Moses also asked God why He would give the Egyptians reason to say that God brought His people out of bondage, only to kill them in the wilderness. Finally, Moses reminded God of His covenant with Abraham, Isaac, and Israel—that He would multiply their seed as the stars in the sky and bring them to the land He had promised them.

In all these ways, Moses acknowledged that all that was done for the people was by the hand of the only true God. God withheld His wrath.

When Moses arrived at the bottom of the mountain and saw for himself what Aaron and the people had done, he was full of anger. He knew they needed a firm reminder that God and God alone had delivered them from bondage and would by his own power take them into the Promised Land.

Exodus 32:20 shares how Moses burned the calf in the fire and ground it into powder. He threw the powder across the water and made the people drink it.

When we give in to self-will and our own desires, and do not look after the weightier matters of the Kingdom, we will eat that which God intends for blessing, and it will become only waste.

CHAPTER 4

Out of the Fire

WHEN MOSES CONFRONTED AARON about what caused him to bring such sin upon the people, Aaron lied. He tried to still Moses's anger by telling him how the people pressed him to make them gods to go before them. This much was true, but then Aaron told Moses that he took all the gold the people brought him and threw it into the fire. He claimed that when he threw the gold into the fire, out came the calf. Yet Exodus 32:4 is clear that Aaron fashioned the calf with the graving tool, and verse 35 refers to it as "the calf which Aaron made."

Aaron did not want to acknowledge his role in using the fire because his action went against the ways and word of God. The fire of God is meant to produce godly results.

Three Tests of Our Character

In the Bible, fire represents God's presence and marks His dwelling space or temple. Since 1906, for more than a century, we have witnessed many outbreaks of the "fire" of Pentecost. In most cases, these great revivals started with one person who was hungry for more of our Lord Jesus.

William Seymour, a Holiness Pentecostal preacher with a passion to be used by God, launched the fire-filled Azusa Street Revival, a Pentecostal revival meeting that took place in Los Angeles, California, in 1906. This fire spread around the nation and other parts of the world, resulting in a rise in the Pentecostal movement. Major Pentecostal groups were birthed, such as the Church of God, United Pentecostal, Assembly of God, and Foursquare Church. In addition, many independent Pentecostal churches and smaller denominations have come to be.

This is what the fire of God produces, yet Aaron claimed his fire produced a golden calf to be celebrated and revered as a god.

Out of the fire of God will come three tests of our character: the lust of the flesh, the lust of the eyes, and the pride of life.

"For all that *is* in the world, the lust of the flesh, and the lust of the eyes, and the pride of life, is not of the Father, but is of the world."
—1 John 2:16 (KJV)

When we show faith, perseverance, and love/loyalty by fleeing from these worldly things, it refines our character, the way fire refines silver and gold, revealing their purity and value.

Satan tried to lure Jesus into succumbing to those worldly sins—and of course He passed all three character tests.

Luke 4:1 tells us, "And Jesus being full of the Holy Ghost [*and fire*] returned from Jordan, and was led by the Spirit into the wilderness" (KJV, parenthetical phrase added). He was led into the wilderness—the same place Aaron and Israel were while Moses was on the mountaintop, awaiting the written word of God.

Jesus fasted in the wilderness for forty days, and when those days ended, "he afterward hungered" (Matt. 4:2, ASV).

The devil showed up and said to Jesus, "If thou be the Son of God, command that these stones be made bread" (Matt. 4:3, KJV).

Jesus responded, "It is written..." (Matt. 4:4, KJV). This was a test of the lust of the flesh.

Satan then showed Jesus the kingdoms of the world and offered them in all their glory to Jesus if only He would worship him. Again, Jesus's reply was, "It is written..." That was the test of the lust of the eyes.

Finally, the devil took Jesus to Jerusalem, set Him on a pinnacle of the temple, and said to Him, "If thou be the Son of God, cast thyself down from hence." (Luke 4:9, KJV).

Jesus responded: "It is said, Thou shalt not tempt the Lord thy God" (Luke 4:12, KJV).

Notice Jesus used the word "said" in denying this third temptation to succumb to the pride of life, referring to those things spoken by God.

Scripture makes it evident that Jesus was, and remains, full of the fire of God. Revelation 1:14 (KJV) says, "...even his eyes were as a flame of fire." It was this fire that provoked the enemy to test Jesus's character, and he will do the same in our lives. But Jesus held fast to both the *logos* (the written Word of God) and to the *rhema* (God's spoken Word.) By doing so, He stood firm against these temptations, and the fire was able to produce what God intended for Jesus's life.

If we remain continually filled with the fire, with a true passion for the Lord and His Word, it will do the same for us. The fire will produce the anointing, the strength, and the blessing that God has planned for us.

We Must Keep Pride from Extinguishing the Fire

Many long-term ministries exist as a result of the fire. However, while some are healthy and strong, others now walk with a limp. Others have built their own kingdoms while disguising their efforts as doing all only for the Kingdom of God.

Pride can easily creep in as God sends growth and blessing. We can easily forget that it is God's power and anointing at work, not our own. Pride often slips in slowly, and we don't even realize it is taking us over. We don't recognize that how we act and what we say don't always reflect what's in our hearts. At one time, we meant those words, but pride can cause us to speak them only from habit or in a way that keeps people coming for more.

Pride can easily creep in as God sends growth and blessing.

I have a long-term ministry. I was saved at age fifteen and received the fire of Holy Spirit in baptism at age eighteen, after tarrying in the presence of God until close to midnight. It was one of the most powerful experiences of my life. At the service, others told me that I flew backward about 15 feet, hit the wall, slid down it, and then sat on the floor for more than an hour with stammering lips. I remained drunk in the Spirit for another entire day.

The very next Sunday at church, Holy Spirit used me to interpret a prophetic message given in tongues. I heard God's voice clearly for every word.

My calling, and that of many others, is to the office of a prophet. Learning to walk in the prophetic has been a long journey that continues to this day. I have made many mistakes along the way, and I by no means have reached a place of perfection. I am still learning, still growing, and with the fire of God still burning in my heart, I continue to go higher in God and experience greater things.

Regardless of the call or purpose God has given you, the same type of experience in learning your gift can happen to you, and it is God's will for you that it does.

I do not say this to boast of myself, for without God I can do nothing. I say it only to impress upon you that this writing is not of my own doing; it is an urgent word from the Lord.

Habakkuk shares these words:

"I will stand upon my watch, and set me upon the tower, and will watch to see what he will say unto me, and what I shall answer when I am reproved. And the LORD

answered me, and said, Write the vision, and make *it* plain upon tables, that he may run that readeth it. For the vision *is* yet for an appointed time, but at the end it shall speak, and not lie: though it tarry, wait for it; because it will surely come, it will not tarry."
—Habakkuk 2:1–3, KJV

As Holy Spirit brought this vision before me and then continued to expound on the message, He impressed upon me that He chose this time. We are entering a time of prophetic correction to prepare His people for the end-time wealth transfer.

CHAPTER 5

Removing the Dross

In the first two chapters of Amos, we find prophecy of the fire of God coming in judgment.

Israel is called by name beginning in Amos 2:6, and her transgressions are identified. The first mentioned is that Israel sold the righteous for silver and the poor for a pair of shoes; her people panted after the dust of the earth on the heads of the poor.

"Thus saith the LORD; For three transgressions of Israel, and for four, I will not turn away *the punishment* thereof; because they sold the righteous for silver, and the poor for a pair of shoes; That pant after the dust of the earth on the head of the poor..." —Amos 2:6–7 (KJV)

This is a picture of greed and a lack of concern for the poor—a depraved Israel. The wealthy wanted everything the poor had, even to the extent of the dirt and ashes they would put on themselves in times of mourning. Their attitude was, "Who cares if people are suffering, as long as I can continue to gain from their loss?"

Israel's people were successful but lacked moral character. They used outward acts of piety to conceal the motives of their hearts, which included the lusts of the flesh.

Fire Purifies and Refines

Zechariah paints the picture of the refining properties of the fire of God. In Zechariah 13:9 (KJV), God declares, "I will bring the third part through the fire, and will refine them as silver is refined, and will try them as gold is tried." This verse compares the refining process of God's people to the method used to refine gold and silver in fire.

When the gold is being heated in the fire, the impurities, known as *dross*, are forced from the gold and rise to the top of the basin. If the dross is not removed, it dulls the luster of the gold. The gold will not shine as it should.

"Thy silver is become dross, thy wine mixed with water: Thy princes are rebellious, and companions of thieves: every one loveth gifts, and followeth after rewards: they judge not the fatherless, neither doth the cause of the widow come unto them. Therefore saith the Lord, the Lord of hosts, the mighty One of Israel, Ah, I will ease me of mine adversaries, and avenge me of mine enemies: And I will turn my hand upon thee, and purely purge away thy dross, and take away all thy tin: And I will restore thy judges as at the first, and thy counsellors as at the beginning: afterward thou shalt be called, The city of righteousness, the faithful city. Zion shall be redeemed with judgment, and her converts with righteousness." —Isaiah 1:22-27 (KJV)

The Lord spoke to me: "If the impurities are not removed, the luster turns into lust for the gold, which is then kept in the basin (the person) for his or her own use. Eventually, it transforms into a golden calf that is worshipped. The dross becomes the dung from the calf."

The person is still in the fire but does not become

The person is still in the fire but does not become who he or she is intended to be.

who he or she is intended to be. People allow the uncleanness to cleave to themselves instead of allowing the fire to purge them of sin and make them totally pure in the presence of God.

We can only remove what we can see. God does not make us guess. He is not the author of confusion.

The Fivefold Ministry Keeps the Fire from Becoming Lukewarm

As we meditate on His Word and seek His face, He reveals to us those areas of our lives that are clean and those areas He is attempting to purge from our hearts and lives. We can turn a blind eye and refuse to see the impurities. We often do this by isolating ourselves from the "fivefold ministry" as a whole.

This term refers to the five different roles, or ministries, that God has given to believers to equip us for service to Him as we build up the body of Christ. As stated in Ephesians 4:11, these roles are apostles, prophets, evangelists, pastors, and teachers.

When we work as a unit, the fivefold brings correction. But when we ignore the fivefold ministry, we think we are hiding our motives and actions when we are actually rebelling against the corrective ways of God. When we do so, we can put ourselves into grave danger, not only of missed blessings here on earth, but also of the judgment fire of God.

Consider the Laodicean church:

"And unto the angel of the church of the Laodiceans write; These things saith the Amen, the faithful and true witness, the beginning of the creation of God; I know thy works, that thou art neither cold nor hot: I would thou wert cold or hot. So then because thou art lukewarm, and neither cold nor hot, I will spue thee out of my mouth. Because thou sayest, I am rich, and increased with goods, and have need of nothing; and knowest not that thou art wretched, and miserable, and poor, and blind, and naked: I counsel thee to buy of me gold tried in the fire, that thou mayest be rich; and white raiment, that thou mayest be clothed, and that the shame of thy nakedness do not appear; and anoint thine eyes with eyesalve, that thou mayest see. As many as I love, I rebuke and chasten: be zealous therefore, and repent. Behold, I stand at the door, and knock: if any man hear my voice, and open the door, I will come in to him, and will sup with him, and he with me. To him that overcometh will I grant to sit with me in my throne, even as I also overcame, and am set down with my Father in his throne. He that hath an ear, let him hear what the Spirit saith unto the churches." —Revelation 3:14–22 (KJV)

This letter is written to a pre-tribulation church. Jesus tells them that because they have become lukewarm, He will vomit them from His mouth. If they are in His mouth, that means they know His Word and His prophetic voice. They speak His Word and live outwardly according to that Word. But because they have not allowed the fire of God to purify them, they have become lukewarm.

Their passion was no longer for the things of God, but for wealth and riches. They saw themselves as rich because they increased in wealth and material goods. They became self-sufficient and prideful, declaring their need for nothing.

They could not know how wretched, miserable, poor, blind, and naked they really were. God implored them to take only gold purified by the fire; only then would they be truly rich. He told them to use eye salve to clear their blurred vision so they could see who they really were compared to who they were meant to be.

They were unaware of the dross. They did not see the dung of the golden calf smeared on their clothing.

The Challenges to Avoid Impropriety Continue Today

Let's briefly review the key events in the Bible that show how God's people have struggled with impropriety.

As mentioned earlier, in the days of Aaron, the people sought gods to expedite their arrival into their Promised Land, where they would enjoy blessings and riches. Aaron the priest not only condoned their desires but fashioned the golden calf for them to worship. He celebrated along with the people in agreement that their own way of achieving their desires was better than God's.

Then, in the days of Amos, God spoke of judgment to come upon Israel, who had become so full of lust for money that her people didn't care whom they had to hurt or oppress to get it.

Centuries later, Jesus addressed the church of Laodicea, exposing their poor and wretched condition when they thought they were rich. Their thinking resulted in their eyes being blinded to the effects of the impurities in their lives that surfaced when they made wealth and riches their god.

Two thousand years later, these trends, these improprieties, unfortunately remain a part of many ministries.

The methods may not look exactly the same, but the works are the same.

Unsatisfied with the timing and blessings of God, ministers devise their own means of expediting notoriety and financial gain. Their view is that, if that means pressuring the poor to give beyond their means and making them feel like God won't bless them unless they do, so be it. All the while, they see themselves as rich, when they are actually poor, naked, and blind. They see themselves as clean, unaware their backsides are covered with dung.

Over the past forty years, a generation, we have witnessed the downfall of many as a result of the dross. This has occurred in both small and mega-ministries to some who have made the golden calf in their basin from gold they kept covered. They have allowed impurities to remain, causing the flame to die down in their spirits, to become lukewarm.

Yet they continue to come to the stage, to the pulpit and platform, and present themselves in such a way that it appears they are producing the fire of God for those who are in need. Many people who desire to have that same fire working in them follow these false prophets so they, too, can produce the results they see coming from the platform. They come, expecting to receive the fiery anointing of God.

Whether to meet a need in their life such as healing or deliverance from a given situation, or whether to increase in the anointing, these people are hungry for the true fire and power of God.

They are often convinced that the only way the fire they desire will come is through their giving. The greater the sacrifice, the greater the return. Some start by giving smaller amounts but are quickly asked for amounts in the thousands of dollars.

The giving escalates. Desperate for the blessings of God, people start offering hundreds and thousands of dollars. They give in the form of jewelry, homes, cars, planes, elaborate vacations, and other such luxuries.

The principle of sowing and reaping in faith is an important doctrine that should be taught to the people. There is no wrong in sowing large amounts of money or goods into Kingdom work.

However, Jesus said, "Freely you have received, freely give" (Matt. 10:8, NKJV). God will not only provide; He will also abundantly bless a fire-filled ministry. Too many ministers have fallen into the enemy's trap, lured there by the lust of the flesh, the lust of the eyes, and the pride of life.

> *They are often convinced that the only way the fire they desire will come is through their giving.*

As a result, they have grown or are growing lukewarm. They have fashioned a golden calf because God isn't blessing them as quickly or to the level they think they deserve, so a price is put on the work of the gospel. I was in service many years ago when there were actually different prayer lines based upon the amount of money the giver put in their envelope. Those in need of prayer could only stand in the line bearing that particular price ($40 line, $100 line, etc.) The higher the amount, the more prayer that person received and the more they could expect from God.

It seems we need to be reminded of God's Word through the prophet, Micah:

"Hear this, I pray you, ye heads of the house of Jacob, and princes of the house of Israel, that abhor judgment, and pervert all equity. They build up Zion with blood, and Jerusalem with iniquity. The heads thereof judge for reward, and the priests thereof teach for hire, and the prophets thereof divine for money: yet will they lean upon the LORD, and say, Is not the LORD among us? none evil can come upon us. Therefore shall Zion for your sake be plowed as a field, and Jerusalem shall become heaps, and the mountain of the house as the high places of the forest." —Micah 3:9–12 (KJV)

A Pastor Brought Back to Life in Africa Tells of the Fire of Judgment

Reinhard Bonnke (1940–2019) was a Pentecostal evangelist who had had been a missionary in Africa since 1967. He once shared an experience that occurred at one of his meetings while in Nigeria in 2001.

A pastor named Daniel Ekechukwu was killed in a car accident, and his body lay in a morgue for three days. His wife, standing on the Word of God, determined to get him to Bonnke's meeting, where the anointing of God would be strong. With help, she got her husband to the meeting. His body was placed in a casket in the basement where the service was being held.

As Bonnke preached, some pastors prayed around Ekechukwu's body. Suddenly, the man began to breathe. He was brought back to life and told the story of all that happened to him while he was dead. He experienced an out-of-body experience with the Lord. I will not tell the whole story here, but I encourage you to review published accounts of this story.[1] It is a powerful testimony that has led many people to the Lord.

I want to address one part of Ekechukwu's testimony. When he was killed, two angels escorted him to Heaven. An angel led him, showing him

---

1 An interview that Pat Robertson of *The 700 Club* conducted with Bonnke is available in an article titled "Reinhard Bonnke Tells of Nigerian Man Raised from the Dead" on the Christian Broadcasting Network (CBN) website, date unknown, https://cbn.com/article/salvation/reinhard-bonnke-tells-nigerian-man-raised-dead. Also, you can view a YouTube video titled "Raised from the Dead" at https://www.youtube.com/watch?v=vASN22uGWo0.

many splendors of heaven and the things God has prepared for His children.

The angel then took Ekechukwe to hell. Among the horrible things he witnessed there was a man who was a pastor on this earth, now tormented in the flames of hell. This pastor cried out, "I only stole money from the church. I'll give it back! Help me return the money!"

In his lifetime, that pastor allowed the dross to form a golden calf—a means of increase that did not include God. He took money meant to further the Gospel and used it for his own preservation and pleasure. Now he is tormented in the fire of judgment, having become just as Micah said in Micah 3:11 (KJV), "...the priests thereof teach for hire, and the prophets thereof divine for money: yet will they lean upon the LORD, and say, *Is* not the LORD among us? none evil can come upon us."

CHAPTER 6

How Will Your Legacy Speak for You?

FIRST TIMOTHY 6:1–19 HAS much to say about those in ministry. As Paul mentors young pastor Timothy, Holy Spirit inspires Paul to give sound, godly instruction.

1 Timothy 6:3–4 (KJV) says, "If any man teach otherwise and does not consent to wholesome words, *even* the words of our Lord Jesus Christ, and to the doctrine which is according to holiness; He is proud...". In verse 5, Paul goes on to say, "Perverse disputings of men of corrupt minds, and destitute of the truth, supposing that gain is godliness: from such withdraw thyself."

The minds of those who believe that godliness is a means of gain are corrupt, and they are destitute of the truth. We are to separate ourselves from these people—withdraw from them.

But godliness with contentment is great gain. For we brought nothing into this world, and it is certain we can carry nothing out (vss. 6–7).

I encourage you to read 1 Timothy 6:1–19. Meditate on it. Digest it. Then ask yourself what you want your legacy to say about you. Would you have it be that you were destitute of the truth and saw godliness and ministry as the means for your own personal gain? Or would you have it said of you that you lived with the great gain of godliness in contentment, trusting God to prosper you according to His will and plan for your life?

Egyptian pharaohs would construct large, elaborate tombs and have all their possessions—sometimes including even their slaves—buried with them.

> *They left nothing behind to serve the people and took their wealth to their graves with them.*

They left nothing behind to serve the people and took their wealth to their graves with them. Many of those possessions wound up in the hands of thieves and grave robbers who would desecrate the tombs to steal the spoil. The pharaohs' legacy, an elaborate pyramid filled with earthly gain, stood as a witness and testimony against them.

Several ministries in the recent past have left such a legacy. Their lifestyle of using godliness as a means for gain was exposed. As a result, they left this world or closed their doors, leaving a legacy that testified against them.

Kathryn Kuhlman: Becoming Who God Wanted Her to Be

There are those, however, who left behind a legacy of godliness to further God's Kingdom. Even though they also acquired great wealth and were followed by the masses, wealth was not their purpose—serving God was. Their ministries continue to change lives today. Just a few of those legacies live through the Moody Bible Institute, John G. Lake Ministries (now led by Curry Blake), the Billy Graham Association, and Oral Roberts University.

These ministers have enjoyed the blessings of God because the blessings were not their god.

One minister in particular who stands out in my mind is Kathryn Kuhlman. Her biography[2] is a source of inspiration to me. It tells of Kathryn coming to the end of herself and becoming who Jesus wanted her to be.

---

2   Jamie Buckingham, *Daughter of Destiny: Kathryn Kuhlman* (Bridge-Logos, Inc., 1969).

When asked about her past, Kathryn would say, "That person no longer exists." She started out flying commercial airlines to her meetings. The story is told how people at one airport would fall out in the Spirit as Ms. Kuhlman walked through the terminal. After this happened several times, the police chief figured out what was happening and started escorting her to the plane using a different route. Eventually, other ministers started sending their private planes to fly her to her destinations, as did at least one mayor of a city anticipating her arrival.

Kathryn Kuhlman brought the fire of God to the people. The power of that fire within her was evident in many signs and wonders. Miracles increased, as did her ministry. Along with that, her wealth increased in the form of jewels, art, expensive clothing, and cash.

It is said that if someone went to her office to criticize her ministry, she would simply say, "Love them, Jesus." Some of these people would then be slain under the power of Holy Spirit and remain there for hours.

With all the power of God that operated through her, with all the notoriety and the wealth, Ms. Kuhlman remained humble before God. She often made mention of the price she paid for her relationship with Jesus and the ministry. "He's all I have," she would say, "and He's all I want."

God honored this heart and stood Kathryn before multitudes of people, both small and great. She went home to be with Jesus in 1976. For forty years, her legacy continued through the Kathryn Kuhlman Foundation, which provided scholarships to Wheaton College, whose motto is "For Christ and His Kingdom." Kathryn's legacy also speaks to the world as she is remembered for her humility, her desire to please Him, and her love for Jesus above all things.

This is the type of legacy you can leave when you have been purified in the fire and the dross has been removed.

The Godly Legacy of Loyce Rowland, My Spiritual Mother and Pastor

I want to share one more example of a steadfast woman of God, although she is much less renowned than Kathryn Kuhlman. Her name is Loyce Rowland, and she was my spiritual mother and mentor. I was saved and filled with Holy Spirit under her ministry, and she guided me into ministry when God showed her the call on my life, that I would receive the gift of prophecy. And I did.

After the death of her husband in 1973, Pastor Rowland continued the ministry on her own. Her church was small, with fewer than one hundred people, but her ministry changed many lives.

She was never wealthy, and she worked full-time during many of her pastoral years. Still, she never went without, and God worked miracle after miracle for her when it was time for her to build a bigger church. She was determined to build it debt-free. When it looked like she could not finish, God laid it on the hearts of business owners in the then-small town to send materials and money. The building was finished without debt.

In 1997, the City of Minneola adopted a Resolution to Proclaim October 26, 1997, as "We Appreciate Pastor Rowland Day." The resolution referred to her as a "silent help," never caring if her name was known or her bank account fat. It cited her services to area hospitals, nursing homes, and jails, stating that she was never known to refuse a call, regardless of the hour. The resolution went on to speak of her honesty and integrity, living a life beyond reproach. Bringing it to a close were these words:

> *Whereas, as a result of her efforts, the residents of Minneola have had someone to go to in times of trouble regardless of sex, race, economic standing, spiritual beliefs or church attendance;*
>
> *Now therefore, be it known that we, the Minneola City Council, appreciate and honor the*

years she has dedicated to the people of this city and the example of love, generosity, and true Christianity that she has set for those around her; and hereby proclaim October 26, 1997 to be recognized as "We Appreciate Pastor Rowland" Day.

What a powerful legacy—to be recognized on behalf of true Christianity, not only by those in the body of Christ, but by the community as a whole. Pastor Rowland went to be with Jesus on October 22, 2024, just one week shy of her ninety-seventh birthday. The response to her death was overwhelming. Hundreds of people from around the country sent their stories of how she led them to the Lord, helped them get started in ministry, or helped them in a time of crisis.

Her legacy continues through at least thirty people still in ministry at some level today, including me. The church she and her husband founded remains, and people continue to have their lives changed by the fire of God through those who have succeeded her. Her legacy demonstrates her commitment to serving the Lord.

Earlier, I mentioned that in my vivid dream in which the Lord spoke to me, He told me she would pass away that same morning. An hour and a half later, I got a call saying she had passed, confirming one of the main points in my dream.

Your legacy will speak on your behalf. Will it tell of pride, materialism, and fame at the expense of the people? Or will it speak of your passion for Jesus and His purpose for your life? I urge you to strive for the latter, for that passion for Jesus and His purpose for your life is the key to participating in the end-time wealth transfer.

CHAPTER 7

The Wealth Transfer: Who Will Be Able to Participate?

GOD CONTINUED TO SPEAK to me about the dream. Though wide awake, I would see it play out again and again before my eyes. He reminded me, "I have tolerated this behavior for the sake of winning souls. The harvest is white, but the workers are few." They are ready to be saved; when it's white, it is ready to be harvested.

On this particular day, the Lord began to explain more to me about His purpose and told me to spread the word. He shared that the often-mentioned wealth transfer will take place more rapidly and at greater levels than ever before, beginning in 2025 and continuing for a season.

The Lord is trying to bring correction to those in the body of Christ, especially those in the five-fold ministry, so that all can participate. If correction does not come with the golden calves, they will be ground into powder. Not only will these people not be able to benefit from the wealth transfer, their already-acquired wealth could be transferred to the more faithful few elsewhere in God's Kingdom.

In Deuteronomy 8, the people are reminded that it was God's power, not their own, that brought them safely through the dangerous wilderness and kept them fed and clothed. They are admonished to remember that is God's power, not their own, that will cause them to prosper with gold, silver, and nice homes in their land. There are consequences if you forget your God:

"And thou say in thine heart, My power and the might of mine hand hath gotten me this wealth. But thou shalt remember the LORD thy God: for it is he that giveth thee power to get wealth, that he may establish his covenant which he sware unto thy fathers, as it is this day. And it shall be, if thou do at all forget the LORD thy God, and walk after other gods,

> and serve them, and worship them, I testify against you this day that ye shall surely perish." —Deuteronomy 8:17–19 (KJV)

Job 21 tells of how the wicked wealthy live days without worry. They prosper and spend their days in song and dance. Job 21:14–155 (KJV) says, "Therefore they say unto God, Depart from us; for we desire not the knowledge of thy ways. What *is* the Almighty, that we should serve him? and what profit should we have, if we pray unto him?"

You might argue here that Job is referring to the wicked wealthy, not those in the kingdom of God. We must acknowledge the fact that even as ministers of the Gospel, when our lack of no need

> *What is the Almighty, that we should serve him? and what profit should we have, if we pray unto him?"*

deceives us into thinking we have no need of our Creator and Provider, wickedness has entered our hearts.

In two different parables, Jesus calls a servant "wicked" (see Matthew 18:32) and "wicked and slothful" (see Matthew 25:26). In both these parables, the servants represent servants of the master or king, yet wickedness was found in their hearts. Matthew 25 is an example of even those in the Kingdom of God having their wealth transferred to another within the kingdom: "Take therefore the talent from him, [the servant who produced nothing for the kingdom] and give *it* unto him which hath ten talents" (Matt. 25:28, KJV, parenthetical comment mine). Sadly, it cost this servant even his soul as he was cast into outer darkness.

The often-referenced Proverbs 13:22b (KJV) tells us, "and the wealth of the sinner *is* laid up for the just." The body of Christ has long identified the sinner in this verse as the unsaved, those with no relationship with Jesus. God spoke to me that those people are only a part of the sinners referenced. The word "sinner" simply means one who sins. We have all sinned and come short of the glory of God, and there are many in the body of Christ who sin against God by allowing self-gain to be their motivation. They see themselves as the ones making it happen, and godliness takes a backseat to wealth and fame. Through repetition of practices they see working for them, they become callous and their ears deaf to the voice of Holy Spirit.

First Timothy 6:10 makes it clear that the love of money is the root of all evil. The word "love" here describes an excessive or inordinate desire of gain. It speaks of a passionate love that results in a greediness for wealth and covetousness. This excessive love for wealth is the root cause of all evil—not Satan, as one might suspect.

Satan showed Jesus all the kingdoms of the world in their glory and said to Jesus, "Just worship me, and I will give you all of this." Too many people who would never knowingly worship Satan are blinded to the fact that he lured them into evil using their love of money and self-preservation as his weapon.

How many have fallen into this trap?

When we become overly confident in our own ability to usher in the presence of Holy Spirit, He will test our relationship with Him. Will we realize the path we are taking is the wrong path, covered in dross? And will we yield ourselves to be purified by the fire on the altar of sacrifice?

Who, then, will be able to participate in the great wealth transfer?

Not those who are described in any of these passages we have just read. It will be those who realize that God and God alone brings the fire, the power, and the increase into our lives. It will be those who will continue earnestly in their work for the Lord, regardless of personal gain. It will be those who understand the necessity of keeping their eyes on the cross of self-sacrifice as the essential element to a fulfilled life and ministry.

CHAPTER 8

The Wealth Transfer: How Will It Happen?

In Luke 17:20 (KJV), Jesus tells us, "The kingdom of God cometh not with observation:" Romans 14:17 adds to this statement with these words: "For the kingdom of God is not meat and drink; but righteousness, and peace, and joy in the Holy Ghost."

We must allow the fullness of Holy Spirit to dwell in us continuously—daily, minute by minute. Galatians 5:16 (KJV) explains the importance of doing so: "This I say then, Walk in the Spirit, and ye shall not fulfil the lust of the flesh."

Remaining constantly full of Holy Spirit and walking with Him is our protection from the temptation to pursue wealth at any cost.

The Lord gave me another vision. I saw Jesus's silhouette seated on the mercy seat. He was radiant, with light flowing all around him. In front of him was an altar roughly seven or eight feet long. In the center of that altar, directly in front of Jesus, was a pulsating flame that hovered over the altar. The flame appeared as an almost-transparent, reddish-colored liquid.

The altar I saw before Jesus was a sacrificial altar, one on which we are to offer ourselves to the Lord.

"I beseech you therefore, brethren, by the mercies of God, that ye present your bodies a living sacrifice, holy, acceptable unto God, which is your reasonable service." —Romans 12:1

Paul is pleading with all believers to live our lives in a continual state of surrender to God, presenting ourselves as a living sacrifice to live a life holy and acceptable to God. This is not some grand or extreme act to be carried out only by the godly elite. It is the reasonable, rational, logical service of every believer.

And it is how Jesus lived. He always did what pleased the Father (see John 8:29).

In Galatians 2:20 (KJV), Paul spoke of himself as being crucified with Christ. He added, "Nevertheless I live; yet not I, but Christ liveth in me: and the life which I now live in the flesh I live by the faith of the Son of God, who loved me, and gave himself for me."

"The wealth transfer will come through this altar of sacrifice," saith the Lord to me.

Let's consider an event in Abram's (Abraham's) life as told in Genesis 15. God tells Abram to "fear not, for I am your shield and your exceeding great reward." He was reassuring Abram that he would protect him and that Abram would be greatly rewarded.

This prompted Abram to ask God how he would be rewarded. He asked, "But what will you give me seeing I go

> *God had already given Abram everything he wanted except a son.*

childless, and the steward of my house is this Eliezer of Damascus?" God had already given Abram everything he wanted except a son. Anything God gave to Abram would be left to his servant.

God reaffirms that Abram will have seed on this earth, as the stars of the sky. Abram believed

God. Then God tells Abram that he brought him out of Ur of the Chaldees so that he would inherit this great land. Abram asked God how he would know that he will inherit the land. God responded by telling Abram to bring a sacrificial offering. He gave Abram specific instructions concerning the sacrifice.

What Abram did next is significant. He killed the sacrificial animals and laid them out on the altar. When the fowl came to devour the carcasses, Abram drove them away to protect the sacrifice.

Not only must our sacrificial lifestyle be continual, we must be truly committed to it. Whether it be time, finances, or some other aspect of our life on that altar, if we are not fully committed to protecting the sacrifice, the devil will be easily able to steal it away. We will soon find ourselves willing to sacrifice less and less, while still expecting the blessing the sacrifice brings.

When the enemy of our sacrifice comes to steal, it will be a test of our commitment. He will try to convince us that just one piece of this or one bit of that missing from the sacrifice won't matter. Don't fall for the lie. Remain strong. Remain committed. Continue to present your body as a living sacrifice.

If we desire the blessing that comes from the altar, our relationship with the Father cannot be half-hearted. The fullness of the covenant comes to those who are consistent and committed to God.

After all of this, an intense darkness fell on Abram, and he slept. There, in the darkness, the sacrifice was consumed by the fire of God, and God entered into covenant with Abram concerning his seed and the land they were to possess.

When remaining at the altar becomes difficult and all seems dark, pray for grace. We all need more of the favor of God. And it may be in this time of difficulty that your blessing and increase will come.

CHAPTER 9

Prophetic Words

So, what does all of this have to do with the transfer coming from the altar? I return to the vision God set before my eyes to explain. I shared already that I saw a flame hovering over the altar that day. As I sat mesmerized by what was before me, the flame started to take action. At various times, the flame would separate and leave the altar, headed in three different directions.

The Lord then spoke these prophetic words to me:

In this next year, saith He that sits on the throne of grace, will come wealth transfers, but not all will receive because many are not willing to be a living sacrifice upon My altar of sacrifice. Many who have gathered wealth from living in the fire on My altar have faltered.

They let their desire to secure for themselves houses in locations all over the world and millions of dollars of wealth in hidden banks, walls, and floors, many cars, jewels, and other things I know of pull them away. This I say: 2024 exposed a few and gave them time for repentance; 2025 will bring them home to Me if they do not change.

The wealth transfer will continue to My disciples and to My fivefold ministry. All is to bring a final transfer before a great falling away. Know this, saith the Holy One of Israel: none can go further than their willingness to be a daily sacrifice for My glory.

Know this: I will bring every work into judgment with every secret thing, whether it be good or whether it be evil.

As I sat listening to the voice of the Lord, He continued to speak to me in a powerful way. He said to me, "Jeremiah 23:24." I turned there quickly to find these words: "Can any hide himself in secret places that I shall not see him? saith the LORD. Do not I fill heaven and earth?" (KJV)

He reminded me of one of the main aspects in the role of prophets by speaking Amos 3:7 (KJV): "Surely the Lord GOD will do nothing, but he revealeth his secret unto his servants the prophets."

The direct prophetic word from the Lord to me then continued:

I know everywhere you have been. I know of the private meeting places where you spent My wealth on extravagant travels and meals above the scenic places of the world. I was and am where you are.

These things are measured, and you are found wanting more than is necessary to carry out your calling. I stand at the door and knock. Why are you not answering? The time is short for many. An encounter is just ahead for many. Watch where you spend My time, My wealth, and My life that is within you before payment is due. It is the account that matters, My servants! Who are you going to be accountable to?

For I say to My servants, cursed be the man that makes any graven or molten image—an abomination unto the Lord and the work of the hands of craftsmen—and puts it in a secret place. For there is no secret that shall be hidden or kept; it shall be noised upon the housetops. My Father that seeth thee in secret shall reward thee openly, good or bad, that thy soul should be saved. I say unto you, lay not up for yourselves treasures upon the earth where moth and rust corrupt and where thieves break through and steal. But lay up for yourselves treasures in heaven, for where your treasure is, there will your heart be. I say unto you, no man can serve two masters. You cannot serve God and mammon.

CHAPTER 10

Penalties for Sin

After that serious warning from the Lord, God dealt with me strongly concerning events in Scripture. He told me these same actions are taking place in the body of Christ today. I am to be reminded, and to remind as many as I can, that penalties follow such behavior.

Gehazi Becomes a Leper as Punishment for Seeking Self-Gain

The first message I bring addresses receiving payment for healing, only to hide it away for oneself. The account is recorded in 2 Kings 5. It is a story full of spiritual principles, but my goal is to focus on the portion that applies to the message of this book—the role of Elisha's servant, Gehazi.

The captain of the host of Syria was a man named Naaman. He was a mighty man of valor, a virtuous man full of honor, power, and wealth. But Naaman was a leper.

Leprosy is a terrible infectious disease that affects the nerves, eyes, and skin. It causes the skin to produce a stench, and over time, the fingers, toes, and ears rot away. Lepers in biblical times had to live apart from other people, in leper colonies or camps.

It so happened that Syria had brought a young maiden captive from Israel, and she was a servant to Naaman's wife. The young lady told Naaman's wife about the prophet Elisha in Samaria and said that Elisha would be able to heal Naaman of his leprosy.

Naaman set out to find Elisha. At the wise counsel of his servants, Naaman reluctantly obeyed Elisha's instructions to receive his healing. The leprosy left Naaman and "... and his flesh came again like unto the flesh of a little child, and he was clean" (2 Kings 5:14, KJV).

Naaman returned immediately to Elisha and offered him blessing—an offering or payment—for the healing. Elisha responded, "As the LORD liveth, before whom I stand, I will receive none" (2 Kings 5:16, KJV). Though Naaman urged Elisha, still Elisha refused and sent Naaman away in peace.

Gehazi came on the scene. He was frustrated that Elisha turned down Naaman's offer and adamantly declared, "As the LORD liveth, I will run after him, and take somewhat of him."

Gehazi caught up to Naaman and told him a lie. He told Naaman that Elisha sent him to get silver and changes of clothing for two sons of the prophets who had come to Elisha. Naaman gladly gave Gehazi two talents of silver and two changes of clothes. Naaman's servants accompanied Gehazi until they reached the tower, where Gehazi took the goods from the two servants and sent them on their way.

I understand that what the KJV states was the tower was actually a fortified hill in Samaria. But as I read this Scripture, the Lord spoke this clearly to me: "I will stand upon My watch, and set Me upon the tower, and will watch to see what he will say unto Me."

God was reminding me of the words of the prophet Habakkuk. What God impressed upon me at that moment applies as if this were the actual tower, and it applies if this were the fortified hill where Gehazi lived. Gehazi left his post. He abandoned his responsibilities and his obedience to his master to go chasing after wealth. He then used this tower as a hiding place so he would not be seen with Naaman's servants. He hid the money inside.

Too many ministers follow this pattern. They neglect seeking God and take their eyes off the purpose of their anointing to pursue wealth their own way. They tell none how they acquired that wealth and hide it away so it will not be exposed. But God sees all.

> *They tell none how they acquired that wealth and hide it away so it will not be exposed. But God sees all.*

The story continues. Gehazi stood before his master, Elisha. Elisha asked Gehazi where he had been, and again Gehazi lied, this time directly to Elisha, saying he didn't go anywhere.

Elisha knew better. He asked Gehazi, "Went not mine heart *with thee*, when the man turned again from his chariot to meet thee? *Is it* a time to receive money, and to receive garments, and oliveyards, and vineyards, sheep and oxen, and menservants and maidservants?" (2 Kings 5:26, KJV).

Elisha then pronounced the penalty: Naaman's leprosy would cleave to Gehazi and his seed forever. Leprosy immediately manifested itself on Gehazi's body, and he left Elisha's presence as a leper.

Here is a question for you to ponder: If on this particular day Gehazi had received only silver and clothing, why did Elisha include orchards, sheep, cattle, and servants in his question to Gehazi?

I believe it is because Elisha's heart had followed Gehazi on other days to other places, where he thought he was secretly building himself an empire. After waiting with patience for Gehazi to repent, the day of reckoning finally came.

We Cannot Hide Anything from God

Our God is patient, merciful, and slow to anger. He said to me that He has allowed much of this behavior to continue for the sake of soul winning. But nothing is hidden from Him. He has been everywhere His servants have been. He has been drawing many to repentance, but they have turned a deaf ear.

There will be penalties if change does not come soon.

> *He has been drawing many to repentance, but they have turned a deaf ear.*

The infection that results in leprosy was, I believe, already inside of Gehazi. It was slowly eating away at his integrity as a true man of God. His focus was on wealth, not true service. When Elisha turned away Naaman's gift, the golden calf appeared, and Gehazi followed after it.

If only Gehazi would have kept his eyes on the true prize and let the love of God and the mercy of Christ keep him, he could have avoided the penalty for his sin. Only Jesus is able to keep us from falling and to present us faultless before the presence of His glory with exceeding joy (see Jude 1:21, 24).

Eli's Sons Die as a Consequence of the Evil Acts He Committed

The next biblical account God brought before me deals with misuse of the Lord's offering. It is the story of the young prophet Samuel and the two sons of the Eli the priest. It is recorded in 1 Samuel, chapter 2.

Samuel's mother, Hannah, was barren. She prayed and told God that if He would give her a son, she would give that son back to Him for His service. When Samuel was old enough, his parents took him to the temple and left him with Eli the priest to be taught and to serve. It is here that chapter 2 begins.

Before I get into the story, I want to share with you just a bit of Hannah's prophetic prayer she prayed that day. Hers was a prayer of rejoicing, in which she declared many works of the Lord, including these:

"The LORD maketh poor, and maketh rich: he bringeth low, and lifteth up. He raiseth up the poor out of the dust, and lifteth up the beggar from the dunghill, to set them among princes, and to make them inherit the throne of glory: for the pillars of the earth are the LORD'S, and he hath set the world upon them." —1 Samuel 2:7–8 (KJV)

It is the Lord that makes people rich, and the Lord that makes people poor. It is He who will lift us up in due season if we keep ourselves humble before Him. He is the great blesser of those who walk uprightly before Him. We err when we allow pride and greed to set in and seek these things in our own way and for the wrong reasons.

Now on to our story. Eli's sons were wicked and did not know the Lord. The Bible calls them "sons of Belial." In the New Testament, this term is used to represent the personification of evil. They would take the best part of the offering, even that portion meant for the offerer and his family. They would mandate how the offering was to be presented to them, even if it went against God's instructions. If the person resisted, Eli's sons would take the offering by force.

"Wherefore the sin of the young men was very great before the LORD: for men abhorred the offering of the LORD." —1 Samuel 2:17 (KJV)

The people told Eli about the many sins his sons committed against Israel—against the very ones they were to minister to. Eli rebuked them and cautioned them to stop because they were sinning against the Lord. The sons did not listen to Eli or change their ways, but Eli took no further action to stop them. A man of God came to Eli with a message from the Lord. These words were included in that message:

"Why then do you kick [trample upon, treat with contempt] My sacrifice and My offering which I commanded, and honor your sons above Me by fattening yourselves upon the choicest part of every offering of My people Israel?" —1 Samuel 2:29 (AMP)

The penalty was pronounced. The two sons, Hophni and Phinehas, would die on the same day. The fulfillment of this prophecy is recorded in 1 Samuel 4:11. Eli and his seed would be removed from the high priesthood. Those who did not die would live in poverty, begging the faithful high priest for even the smallest piece of silver and morsel of bread. The ark of God was taken, and the shout of victory was gone.

It is not wise to misuse the Lord's offerings for self-gain. God allotted ample portions for the priests, but that was not enough for Eli's sons.

They wanted more, the best. They took it without regard to God's word or holy living. They exerted undue pressure and demands on the people, and they paid the price.

It did not have to be that way. Let me point out some invaluable words spoken by the prophet who was sent to Eli. God said, "for them that honour me I will honour..." (vs. 30). In verse 35 (KJV), God speaks through the prophet: "And I will raise me up a faithful priest, that shall do according to that which is in mine heart and in my mind: and I will build him a sure house..."

God Himself will honor and build up the house of those who are faithful to Him. He will bestow blessing upon blessing upon those who have set their hearts and minds to elevating Jesus, not themselves.

God Honors Those Who Honor Him

In 2 Samuel 12 is the story of God sending Nathan the prophet to rebuke David for his sin with Bathsheba. Listen carefully to what God says to David in verse 8:

> "And I gave thee thy master's house, and thy master's wives into thy bosom, and gave thee the house of Israel and of Judah; and *if that had been too little, I would moreover have given unto thee such and such things.*" —2 Samuel 12:8 (KJV, emphasis added)

God is a rewarder of those who diligently seek him (see Hebrews 11:6). For the LORD God is a sun and shield: the LORD will give grace and glory: *no good thing will he withhold from them that walk uprightly* (from Psalm 84:11, emphasis added).

If only each of us could learn to live sacrificially for the glory of God and the expansion of His Kingdom. If only we would learn to trust Him to know what is good for us and when and how He will bless us with those things. We would then be blessed beyond measure because God honors those who honor Him.

When we become unsatisfied with God's blessing or feel the price too high to pay, we may prosper in material wealth for a season, but the day of reckoning will come.

The Lord is showing Himself mighty to those who are truly His through this transfer of wealth, which is directed to those who have a heart for the will of the Father and live a sacrificial daily life for Jesus.

CHAPTER 11

The Blessing of Abraham

Earlier, I addressed Abraham's commitment to the sacrifice God asked him to bring. He obeyed God's Word and then protected the sacrifice from the fowl that tried to take his gift from the altar.

God came to Abraham (known as Abram at that time) in the darkness, accepted Abraham's sacrifice, and entered into covenant with Abraham concerning his seed and the land that was promised to them.

What I want to address now is the prophetic word God gave to Abraham that night about his seed that would happen before they possessed the promised land. The people would be held captive for four hundred years:

"And he said unto Abram, Know of a surety that thy seed shall be a stranger in a land *that is* not theirs, and shall serve them; and they shall afflict them four hundred years; And also that nation, whom they shall serve, will I judge: and afterward shall they come out with great substance." —Genesis 15:13–4 (KJV)

This prophecy was fulfilled in Egypt, where Israelites served as slaves for four centuries. Then came time for the great exodus, as God delivered His people, and Abraham's seed did indeed come out of bondage with great substance:

"And the children of Israel did according to the word of Moses; and they borrowed of the Egyptians jewels of silver, and jewels of gold, and raiment: And the LORD gave the people favour in the sight of the Egyptians, so that they lent unto them such things as they required. And they spoiled the Egyptians." — Exodus 12:35–36 (KJV)

It was the first great and notable wealth transfer. God provided His people, through this wealth transfer, with enough to sustain them through their journey; to establish themselves with homes, cattle, and commerce in their new land; and to maintain the temple duties and worship.

They came out with the wealth of Egypt but then refused to wait on the Lord to fulfill His Word to lead them to their new home.

Their impatience and unbelief, even after all they saw God do to bring them out, drove them to waste what God intended to give them for a new start. The gold and jewels were gathered and formed into the golden calf, which they were then forced to drink. Their blessing and their legacy were literally consumed upon their own lust.

The good news is that the actions of those delivered from Egyptian bondage did not nullify God's covenant with Abraham or God's promise to bless the seed of Abraham:

"Even as Abraham believed God, and it was accounted to him for righteousness. Know ye therefore that they which are of faith, the same are the children of Abraham. And the scripture, foreseeing that God would justify the heathen through faith, preached before the gospel unto Abraham, saying, In thee shall all nations be blessed. So then they which be of faith are blessed with faithful Abraham."
—Galatians 3:6–9 (KJV)

Many people hold fast to this promise because Abraham was very rich in cattle, silver, and gold (see Genesis 13:2). We should hold fast to it because it is the Word of God, and it reflects His will for His children.

However, we too often overlook that we are blessed *with* faithful Abraham. That word "with" denotes union. Let's think about that. Abraham left everything he knew behind to follow God. He was even willing to sacrifice his own son, if necessary, knowing that if he were obedient, God was able to raise his son of promise from the dead. Abraham believed God and was called the friend of God (see James 2:23).

Abraham didn't serve God only for what God would give him. As a friend of God, Abraham's goal was a relationship with God wherein God was glorified. He was willing to do whatever necessary to honor God and show God that he believed in Him, regardless of how things might have looked at the moment.

Abraham wasn't perfect. But he was faithful and obedient. That is why God promised to bless Abraham's seed. "And in thy seed shall all the nations of the earth be blessed; because thou hast obeyed my voice." (Gen. 22:18, KJV).

Many are in union with Abraham. They serve sacrificially and obey the voice of the Lord. God has blessed them and continues to bless them in great ways. The blessing will increase in this coming season of wealth transfer.

Unfortunately, many others are as Abraham's seed in the wilderness. They see only delay in the blessing they think they deserve. They left their altar of sacrifice to pursue wealth and fame without regard to God's Word or plan for their lives. They will not enjoy the benefit of the wealth transfer. Also, they may very well have that

They see only delay in the blessing they think they deserve.

which they have accumulated ground into dust as the golden calves are exposed.

Let's determine to remain in union and be blessed with faithful Abraham.

CHAPTER 12

Where Do We Go from Here?

I BELIEVE WE ALL want to be on the receiving end of the end-time wealth transfer. So, what do we do? Let's review.

Another vision I was given was of Jesus sitting on the mercy seat. His fiery eyes added to the pulsating flame on the altar in front of Him. As I watched, I heard Him say, "Present your body as a living sacrifice, holy and acceptable unto Me. This is your reasonable service." He then told me the transfer will come to those who are willing to live in the fire upon His altar.

Many flock to meetings to experience the fire of the Holy One. Many want to be a carrier of that fire to others. How many, though, are willing to live and set the example of a sacrifice that has been washed with pure water from the inside out?

One requirement of the Levitical priests when preparing the sacrificial animal for the burnt offering was to wash the inward parts of the bullock and its legs with pure water. No other liquid, such as wine, could be added because the water represented the purity of Jesus (and His Word), which is the only thing that can truly cleanse us on the inside.

Jewish historians note that the priests would wash the inward parts of the animal at least three times to make sure they were cleansed properly. A complete cleansing was required because this water was to wash away all the lusts of the flesh. It was to remove every spot of sin so the people could continue in a life clean before God.

Ephesians 5:2 and 5:25 both tell us that Jesus gave Himself an offering and a sacrifice for us so that "he might *sanctify and cleanse it with the washing of water by the word,* That he might present it to himself a glorious church, not having spot, or wrinkle, or any such thing; but that it should be holy and without blemish." (Eph. 5:26–27, emphasis added).

Also in that chapter, we are given a glimpse of how a sacrifice that remains washed in the water will live:

"But fornication, and all uncleanness, or covetousness, let it not be once named among you, as becometh saints; Neither filthiness, nor foolish talking, nor jesting, which are not convenient: but rather giving of thanks. For this ye know, that no whoremonger, nor unclean person, nor covetous man, who is an idolater, hath any inheritance in the kingdom of Christ and of God. Let no man deceive you with vain words: for because of these things cometh the wrath of God upon the children of disobedience. Be not ye therefore partakers with them. For ye were sometimes darkness, but now *are ye* light in *the* Lord: walk as children of light." —Ephesians 5:3–8 (KJV)

Walk as children of light. If you struggle to understand the importance of these words, there is Scripture that might explain why. Speaking of Jesus, John 1:4–5 (KJV) reads, "In him was life; and the life was the light of men. The light shineth in darkness; and the darkness comprehended it not."

The darkness represents evil and spiritual ignorance. Included in the darkness, then, would be the love of money, which is the root of all evil. It is possible that this dark, excessive desire for money and self-gain is yet hovering over your heart and mind. When that happens, it can be difficult to see and comprehend God's will for your life, and the dross that remains can form a "golden calf."

The Lord spoke to me emphatically, "I am not going to tolerate the dung smeared on and following my servants in 2025 and the seasons beyond."

The great wealth transfer that is about to be initiated is going to be awesome. It will be limited in the lives where there is a lack of commitment to Jesus and his purpose. On the flip side, there will be no shortage for those who are committed to the altar and are willing to carry their cross daily.

> *The great wealth transfer that is about to be initiated is going to be awesome.*

Here is a word of advice to those in the five-fold ministry, as well as loyal laity who will also receive: Be quick to liberally distribute excess for the furtherance of the Gospel. Be diligent, fervent, and passionate to serve for the glory of God, not just to make a name for yourself or prove who you are.

A false balance is an abomination to God. It is God's will that you prosper and be in health, even as your soul prospers. The blessings of the Lord make us rich, and He adds no sorrow to it.

I have brought to you the Word of the Lord as He gave it to me. I again stress that He wants each one of us to pay attention, examine ourselves, and repent of anything in our lives that will prevent us from being able to receive wealth in the amazing days ahead. I pray it will be so for all of us. Let Jesus's words take root:

"And Jesus answered and said, Verily I say unto you, There is no man that hath left house, or brethren, or sisters, or father, or mother, or wife, or children, or lands, for my sake, and the gospel's, But he shall receive an hundredfold now in this time, houses, and brethren, and sisters, and mothers, and children, and lands, with persecutions; and in the world to come eternal life. But many *that are* first shall be last; and the last first." —Mark 10:29–31 (KJV)

On the pages that follow, I have included a few items for further thought. I hope you will spend some time on those pages and meditate on them often.

God bless you.

Open Your Heart to a New Level of Sacrifice

IN CONCLUSION, THE PROPHETIC word I have shared with you here is what the Lord said will transpire, in a broad sense, for people who are willing to become living sacrifices for the Kingdom of God.

The Lord has spoken to me about what is coming. He is revealing that people who sacrifice their personal desires to follow God's Perfect Will for their lives will discover hidden wealth around the world in various forms.

A Traditional View of Hidden Wealth

Traditionally, the discovery of "hidden wealth" has related to people finding valuable minerals and gemstones buried in the ground.

For example, in 1842, a gold nugget weighing almost 80 pounds, named "Great Triangle," was found in Russia. The largest gold nugget ever found weighed 220 pounds and was named "Welcome Stranger." Two men discovered the giant nugget in Moliagul, Victoria, Australia, in 1858. Here in the United States, a gold nugget weighing almost 106 pounds was discovered in 1869; it was named the "Monumental Nugget."[3] In 2023, a 55.22-carat ruby was found in Mozambique. It is the largest gem-quality ruby ever found, and in 2024, sold for $34.8 million.[4]

With these discoveries, God has allowed men to uncover hidden wealth in regions all over the world.

---

3   "The World's 30 Largest Gold Discoveries," Gold Industry Group, https://www.goldindustrygroup.com.au/news/2020/11/20/the-worlds-30-largest-gold-discoveries.

4 "The World's Largest Ruby Just Sold for $34.8M. What Does That Tell Us About Demand for Coloured Gems?" Luxury Society, https://luxurysociety.com/en/worlds-largest-ruby-just-sold-348m-what-does-tell-us-about-demand-coloured-gems/.

How the End-Time Wealth Transfer Could Manifest

The end-time wealth transfer could certainly lead God's faithful followers to unearth more valuable minerals and gemstones. However, it also will bring wealth to them in more contemporary forms, such as different measures of investments, enhanced creativity leading to inventions, and new money-making ideas. This wealth will come to those who will sacrifice themselves for the benefit of His Kingdom. The sinner who continues in disobedience to the call of a living sacrifice shall lose the wealth they have to the ones who first seek the Kingdom of our God.

Daniel 12:4 (AMP) says, "Many will go back and forth *and* search anxiously [through the scroll], and knowledge [of the purpose of God as revealed by His prophets] will [greatly] increase." Many now are running to every minister, trying to find the right anointing to get under the minister who has paid a price, of sacrifice, to get something for which they did not sacrifice.

"And you shall remember the LORD your God, for *it is* He who gives you power to get wealth, that He may establish His covenant which He swore to your fathers, as *it is* this day." —Deuteronomy 8:18 (NKJV)

Open Your Heart to a New Level of Sacrifice

Now that you have read this prophetic word from the Lord our God, you know how critical it is to develop a sacrificial life in Christ Jesus. Once you do that, wealth will begin coming to you in the form of opportunities. Get ready for a great journey!

I am persuaded, by experience, that as you open your heart to a new level of sacrifice, for His Kingdom, you will experience increase in your life. He who holds the secrets to wealth has promised this, by covenant in Jesus our Lord, Whom I stand before in His Kingdom.

Start your journey, and never look back. *Wealth cometh in Him!*

Food for Thought

THE FOLLOWING COMMENTS AND Scriptures provide additional instruction for God's followers as we prepare to receive the end-time wealth transfer that He has already set in motion.

Prophecies for Us to Heed

The following are prophecies the Lord has conveyed to me so I can share them with you. These are not my words; I am merely a scribe for Him:

> *Yea, saith the Holy One of Israel, all in my Kingdom have the ability to receive in any place, and city, wherever you are. My arm is not short, nor My ear deaf.*

> *I will give some thirty, some sixty, and some one hundred-fold this lifetime. Those who receive one hundred-fold will be persecuted, and they must understand the increase will be for my Kingdom, not their own. I will give the one hundred-fold only to those who take up their cross and follow Me—to those who are a living sacrifice to Me, called and chosen. They*

will have a pure heart for My people who have lost their way and have slipped away from My houses of worship.

There is only one true anointing: Holy Spirit. There are diversities within that anointing that set My servants in positions for such a time as this.

The next four years, should I tarry, will see a whirlwind of many things moving in and out of the kingdoms of this world. You, my sons and my Esthers, must walk in My peace, be at peace, and seek peace for yourselves and for others.

Do not get lost in wealth gathering or hoarding. The ground of a certain rich man brought forth plenty. As it says in My Word, with no room to bestow his goods, he said, "This will I do: I will pull down my barns and build greater; and there will I bestow all my fruits and my goods" (Luke 12: 18, NKJ).

The Lord thy God said unto him, "Thou fool. This night shall thy soul be required of thee, then whose shall these things be?"

So shall he be that lays up treasure for himself and is not rich toward me, saith God.

Questions to Ask

When the human mind hears a question, it goes searching for an answer. Our spirits do the same. God invites us in Isaiah 1:18, "Come, let us reason together." He wants us to talk to Him about things and learn from Him. The key is to search for the answers in the right place and not presume we already know it all. The answers are found in the written Word of God, and they are revealed to us as we commune with Holy Spirit.

I have listed some questions below that I believe will serve as a safeguard for us against a "golden calf," provided we ask them continuously and seek God's answers, not our own. Some of these questions are answered directly in the written Word and apply to everyone. The answers to other questions will vary from person to person and from situation to situation, based on God's perfect will and plan. This is why it is imperative for us to seek God's answer each time a new situation, opportunity, or temptation concerning wealth and prosperity arises.

Make it a habit to ask questions such as these:

1. Who is to take up their cross and follow Jesus?
2. Who is to present themselves a living sacrifice?
3. Who is to receive from the transfer of wealth?

4. How much of the wealth do I keep for my-self and my family?
5. What portion or percentage of this wealth is the Lord's?
6. If I am to serve portions to other people or works, to whom would that be, and how much?
7. Must I give all to the needs of others, or might I also enjoy the blessing of God?
8. What is Holy Spirit telling me to do in this situation?
9. Who is accountable?
10. Whom do I serve—God or mammon (ma-terial wealth)?

God Wants to Prosper His Children

Psalm 35:27 tells us that God has pleasure in the prosperity of His servant. God has purposed wealth for the body of Christ for several reasons. Here are a few:

- To care for those in full-time ministry and their families
- To sow into the Kingdom of God so the Gospel can continue to go forward. This, of course, takes money.
- To carry out whatever call God has placed on our lives. Our work for the Lord should not be hindered by lack when we serve a

God that supplies all our need by Christ Jesus according to His riches in glory.

- So that we are the head, not the tail. God does not want us to fall under the oppression or control of others who have wealth.
- To help others
- To enjoy

God wants us to enjoy all the freedom prosperity can bring. He simply wants us to remember what's most important so we stay in proper balance. He wants us to trust Him to provide for us according to His plan for our lives as we live sacrificially before Him.

If the wealth, fame, and pleasures of this life become our goal, we will not only risk forfeiting the blessing; we will also grieve the heart of God. Below, I have listed several well-known Scriptures that speak of God's plan to prosper His people. In each one, I have added emphasis to the parts too many people neglect—the connection between our relationship with God and the level of prosperity we enjoy.

Meditate on these often. Examine yourself as you meditate. Don't allow the condemning voice of the enemy to speak, but do listen to the merciful voice of Holy Spirit when He tries to reveal something in your life that needs to change. His grace is sufficient!

"The young lions lack and suffer hunger; But *those who seek the Lord* shall not lack any good thing." —Psalm 34:10 (NKJV)

"*Delight yourself also in the Lord*, and He will give you the desires and secret petitions of your heart." —Psalm 37:4 (AMP)

"For the Lord God is a sun and shield: the Lord will give grace and glory: no good thing will he withhold *from them that walk uprightly*." —Psalm 84:11 (KJV)

"Blessed is the man *who fears the Lord, Who delights greatly in His commandments.* His descendants will be mighty on earth; The generation *of the upright* will be blessed. Wealth and riches will be in his house, And his righteousness endures forever." —Psalm 112:1–3 (NKJV)

"*Honor the Lord with your possessions, And with the firstfruits of all your increase;* So your barns will be filled with plenty, And your vats will overflow with new wine." —Proverbs 3:9–10 (NKJV)

"I love those who love me And those who seek me diligently will find me. Riches and honor are with me, Enduring riches and righteousness. My fruit is better than gold, yes, than fine gold, And my revenue than choice silver. I traverse the way of righteousness, In the midst of the paths of justice, That I may cause *those who love me* to inherit wealth, That I may fill their treasuries." —Proverbs 8:17-21 (NKJV)

"He that giveth unto the poor shall not lack: but he that hideth his eyes shall have many a curse." —Proverbs 18:27 (KJV)

"But without faith it is impossible to please Him, for he who comes to God must believe that He is, and that He is a rewarder of those who diligently seek Him." —Hebrews 11:6 (NKJV)

"Beloved, I pray that you may prosper in all things and be in health, *just as your soul prospers.*" —3 John 2 (NKJV)

*And Finally

The following two Scriptures summarize, and re-iterate, how we need to prepare for the end-time wealth transfer:

"Let us hear the conclusion of the whole matter: Fear God, and keep his commandments: for this *is* the whole *duty* of man. For God shall bring every work into judgment, with every secret thing, whether *it* be good, or whether it be evil." —Ecclesiastes 12:13–14 (KJV)

"Except the LORD build the house, they labour in vain that build it: except the LORD keep the city, the watchman waketh but in vain." —Psalm 127:1 (KJV)

About the Author

DAN BOYKIN WAS BORN and raised in central Florida. He was saved in his hometown, Minneola, at the age of fifteen and was filled with the baptism of the Holy Ghost at the age of eighteen. He was a musician in a Christian band between the ages of eighteen and twenty, and today he plays four instruments.

In 1979, he enrolled in International Seminary and evangelized while continuing his education. Breakthrough in Dan's ministry came in 1987 while attending Orlando Christian Center under Pastor Benny Hinn. At that time, Dan set himself apart to be alone with the Lord for a twenty-one-day period of fasting and prayer. Near the completion of that fast, the Lord called him to pastor, letting him know that walking the road of a pastor would prepare him for the end-time ministry calling.

Boykin pastored for twenty-five years. With God's help, he transformed a small congregation to a thriving church, averaging more than two hundred in weekly attendance. He also taught extension classes for the seminary, training more than one hundred ministers as he earned his own Master of Theology (ThM) degree and eventually earned a Doctor of Divinity (DD) degree. He became an Assistant Professor at International Seminary and a District Pastor for IPHC Sonshine Network Ministries Central District. While holding these positions, Dan helped establish four churches and trained many pastors.

In 2009, Dan relocated to Orlando. As directed by Holy Spirit, he entered a Prophetic-Healing Ministry. Now he dedicates his time to bringing the voice and gifts of God to help the body of Christ. He has since completed a forty-day fast in pursuit of God's love, power, anointing, and direction. Dan hears the voice of God, both on national and personal levels of prophecy. The presence of God is evident in his ministry through signs, wonders, and the prophetic Word. He encourages those wherever he goes to prepare for their next breakthrough by the grace and power of God.

He resides in Clermont, Florida, where he serves as the prophetic voice for Freedom Christian Fellowship.

Dan's heart is first for God and then for God's people. He ministers with Ezra 5:2 as his motto: "...and with them the prophets of God helping them."

DEAR FRIENDS

I hope you enjoyed this book. If you were inspired by the book, we invite you to ask your friends and relatives to read it as well.

Here are a few ways that you can help us spread the word:

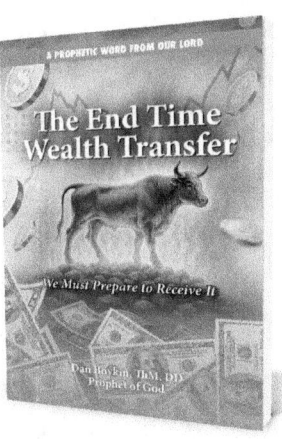

- Recommend the book to friends – word-of-mouth is still the most effective form of advertising.
- Purchase additional copies to give away as gifts on my website.
- Post a 5-Star review on Amazon.
- Write about the book on your Facebook, X, Instagram, LinkedIn—any social media you use!
- If you blog, consider referencing the book, or publishing an excerpt from the book with a link back to my website. You have my permission to do this if you provide proper credit and backlinks.

For more information

Find Dan Boykin and Dan Boykin Ministries on
Facebook by visiting the Dan Boykin Prophetic
Healing Ministries page.

Speaking Engagements

Book Dan Boykin to be a speaker at your next
event by contacting him at these links:

Facebook: Dan Boykin Ministries
(scan the QR code above)

YouTube: www.youtube.com/@danboykin